Fox, Alligator and Rabbit

Retold by Michael Rosen
Illustrated by Mini Goss

CELEBRATION PRESS
Pearson Learning Group

This story was told to Michael Rosen by a thirteen-year-old boy named Jason Broadbent in a London comprehensive school. He was born in Jamaica and his grandmother there told him this story. Stories such as these are of African origin. They were taken to the Caribbean by enslaved Africans, and have been retold in Creole.

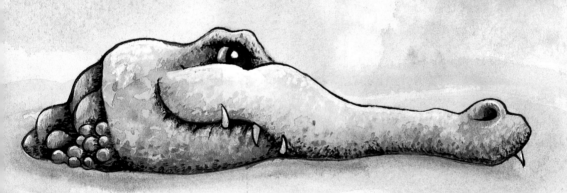

Once there was a fast, wide river. On one side stood a market, and on the other a town. So to get to the market from the town, you had to cross the river. But—and this was a mighty big 'but'—in the middle of the river was Alligator. Now alligators have got their own special way of letting you know they're around—they try and eat you.

One day, Fox and Rabbit wanted to cross the river to the market. Rabbit was working on some kind of a plan.

"Say, Fox," he says, "is it true you foxes are known for being just about the smartest, cleverest creatures around?"

"Yep," says Fox.

"Then how about you taking me across the river?"

"Sure," says Fox, "I'll do it for some of those melons you've got there."

"That's fine," says Rabbit.

"Then you just watch me, Rabbit," says Fox, "and you'll see how to lick this alligator thing, no trouble."

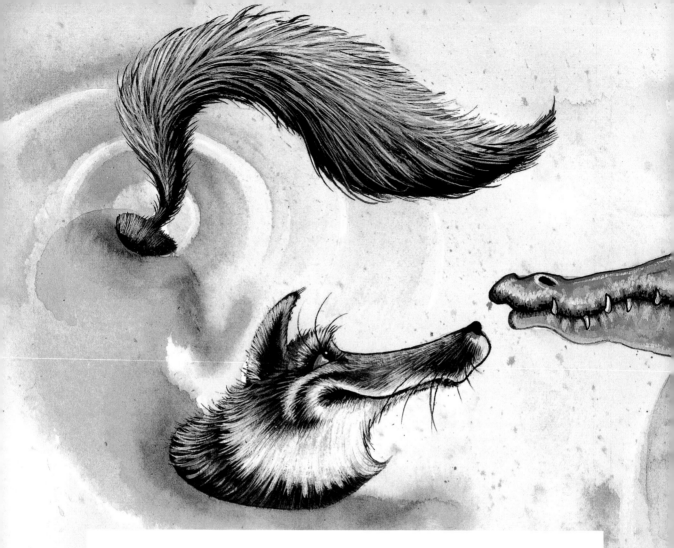

So Fox hightailed out into the river, and you can be sure he knows some things that no one else knows. He knows that Alligator likes his porridge so hot it'd burn your eyelashes to eat it. And another thing—Alligator is stupid. He is so stupid he's been known to think his tail was a fish and give himself a terrible bite. WHEEEEE, that hurt!

So Fox is swimming along and he meets Alligator. One more thing about Alligator, he may be stupid, but believe me, he thinks he's one smart guy.

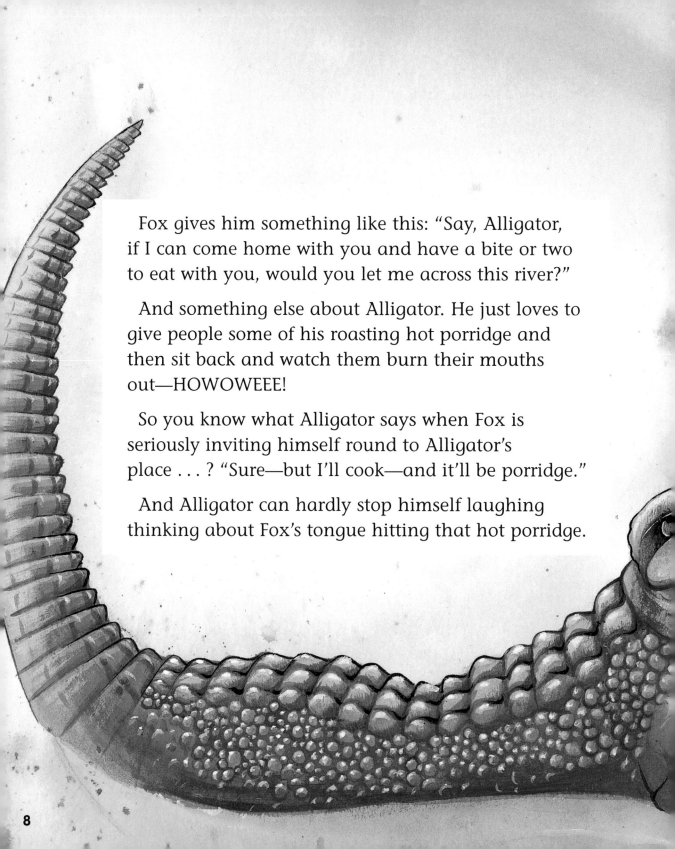

Fox gives him something like this: "Say, Alligator, if I can come home with you and have a bite or two to eat with you, would you let me across this river?"

And something else about Alligator. He just loves to give people some of his roasting hot porridge and then sit back and watch them burn their mouths out—HOWOWEEE!

So you know what Alligator says when Fox is seriously inviting himself round to Alligator's place . . . ? "Sure—but I'll cook—and it'll be porridge."

And Alligator can hardly stop himself laughing thinking about Fox's tongue hitting that hot porridge.

As soon as they get to Alligator's place, Alligator starts cooking the porridge. About two hours later, it's ready and he pours it out into a big, big bowl to eat.

Fox takes his spoon down to the porridge real slow, he lifts it up to his mouth just as slow and then as soon as it hits his tongue he says, "Oooh no, this is much too cold for me, Alligator. Why not put it out in the sun to warm up, huh?"

Alligator loves that. Make it even hotter. Great idea. Then it'll be so hot, Fox won't even be able to bear looking at it. He won't be crossing the river today, thinks Alligator, and he puts the porridge out in the sun.

Two hours later he brings it back in.

"Try that, Fox," says Alligator. He can hardly wait for the screams.

Down goes the spoon real slow, up it comes just as slow and then as soon as it hits Fox's tongue, he says, "Oooh no, it's still too cold. Put it out in the sun for a while more."

So out goes the porridge again, for three hours more. This porridge is going to be awful hot, thinks Alligator. Even I might find it tough getting it down me.

After all this time, the porridge is stone cold.

"I'll give it a try now," says Fox. "I just hope it's hotted up some."

Down goes the spoon real slow, up it comes just as slow and as soon as it hits Fox's tongue he says, "Hey, Alligator, now we are really cooking on all four burners. This is what I call hot. Just give me that porridge." And Fox digs into that porridge like there's no tomorrow.

Believe me, Alligator is impressed. He's sitting there figuring and figuring about how Fox's mouth can take all that burning.

With Fox finished, Alligator says to him, "If you like it that much, Brother, why not have some more?"

"I sure would like to," says Fox, "but I've got business at the market today. I've got to stock up on porridge."

And now Alligator says, "OK. I'll let you get across. It's been a pleasure to see someone like my porridge so much."

"The pleasure's mine," says Fox, and off he swims.

And as he's swimming along, Fox is thinking of those melons Rabbit has promised him. But Alligator's sitting there eating the cold porridge and he's figuring and figuring: How come my porridge is so cold but his porridge was getting hotter? Now that's something I must ask that Fox.

So quick as a fish, Alligator swims after Fox and in two blinks of an eye he's up to him.

"Say, Fox, tell me this, how come your porridge was hotter than mine?"

Sheesh, thinks Fox, he's figured it out. I'd better get these legs moving.

"What's that you say?" says Fox.

"How come your porridge—"

"My what?" says Fox.

"Your porridge."

"My pocket?"

"No, your porridge."

"What about my porridge?"

"How come it was hotter than mine?"

But by now, Fox has made it to the other side and has climbed out onto the bank.

"I'll tell you tomorrow," says Fox and he's off to the market.

When he gets there, what do you know—Rabbit's standing there waiting for him.

"OK, big boy," says Fox, "how come you got across?"

And Rabbit says, "You're not the only one with a bit of sense round here. What do you think I was doing while you were with Alligator?"

At that he slaps his sides and whoops with laughter.

Fox watches him for a while and then says, kind of slow and soft, "So tell me this, Rabbit, if you weren't watching me to see how I got across just then, how are you going to get back?"

Rabbit stops all his laughing right there and then.